BRINGING UP BOYS PARENT WORKBOOK

bringing up boys™

The Video Series

Featuring

DR. JAMES DOBSON

12 Sessions for Parents

DR. JAMES DOBSON'S BRINGING UP BOYS™ PARENT WORKBOOK
FOR THE *DR. JAMES DOBSON'S BRINGING UP BOYS™ PARENTING VIDEOS* SERIES

A Focus on the Family book published by Tyndale House Publishers, Wheaton, Illinois.

Portions of this guide are excerpted with permission from the book *Bringing Up Boys* by Dr. James
Dobson, © 2001 by James Dobson, Inc. All rights reserved. Published by Tyndale House Publishers.

Scripture quotations are from the *Holy Bible*, New International Version ®. NIV®.
Copyright ©1973, 1978, 1984 by the International Bible Society. Used by permission of Zondervan
Publishing House. All rights reserved.

ISBN 1-58997-146-9

Printed in the United States of America

05 06 07 08 09 10/9 8 7 6 5 4 3 2 1

TABLE OF CONTENTS

INTRODUCTION:
how to use this workbook

Welcome!

This book has one aim: to help you get the most from the *Bringing Up Boys*™ video series featuring best-selling author and psychologist Dr. James Dobson. Whether you're watching the series alone or with your spouse, we want the experience to be as educational, experiential, and enriching as possible. Toward this end, we recommend you choose a time during the week to apply the principles of the sessions with your son, spreading out the activities over the course of 12 weeks.

Here's what you'll find in each session:

Quotes and Questions. Read the brief quote from Dr. Dobson's book *Bringing Up Boys*™ (Tyndale House). Then answer the questions that follow it, to help you prepare to watch the video.

Video Journal. As you watch, take notes to help you focus on key concepts. An outline is provided in this section to get you started.

Scriptures to Study. After the video, read over the related Bible passages. The verses are printed in this section for your convenience.

Apply It. In this exercise, you will begin to connect a *Bringing Up Boys* principle with your own experience.

Try It. This section features practical, creative ways to apply what you've learned to your son or sons. Use these tips during the week.

Whether or not you're currently raising boys, whether you're single or married, this series will help you gain plenty of insight into those beguiling, exasperating, priceless creatures made of "snakes, snails, and puppy dog tails." Enjoy the videos—and the boys in your life!

B⚾YS WILL
BE BOYS

Quotes &
Questions

"A boy harasses grumpy dogs and picks up kitties by the ears. His mom has to watch him every minute to keep him from killing himself. He loves to throw rocks, play with fire, and shatter glass. He also gets great pleasure out of irritating his brothers and sisters, his mother, his teachers, and other children. As he gets older, he is drawn to everything dangerous—skateboards, rock climbing, hang gliding, motorcycles, and mountain bikes....It's a wonder any of them survive. Not every boy is like this, of course, but the majority of them are."

—DR. JAMES DOBSON IN THE BOOK
BRINGING UP BOYS (TYNDALE HOUSE)

Do any boys you know fit the above description?

If so, would you change them if you could?
Why or why not?

Video Journal

Use this space to take notes as you watch the video.

"Typical" boy behaviors include…

The "unisex" movement of the 1970s promoted the idea that…

But more recent scientific discoveries have revealed…

In temperament and behavior, males and females are different in these ways…

Our response to "boyish" behavior should be…

Scriptures to Study

"So God created man in His own image, in the image of God He created him; male and female He created them."

—GENESIS 1:27

"When the time drew near for David to die, he gave a charge to Solomon his son. 'I am about to go the way of all the earth,' he said. 'So be strong, show yourself a man, and observe what the LORD your God requires: Walk in His ways, and keep His decrees and commands, His laws and requirements, as written in the Law of Moses, so that you may prosper in all you do and wherever you go, and that the LORD may keep His promise to me: "If your descendants watch how they live, and if they walk faithfully before me with all their heart and soul, you will never fail to have a man on the throne of Israel."'"

—1 KINGS 2:1–4

"Brace yourself like a man; I will question you, and you shall answer Me."

—JOB 38:3

 **Apply It:**

Preschool:

You're at your wit's end with your four-year-old. He's always getting into things. His favorite game is to play racetrack with toy cars—which inevitably ends with a vehicle crashing through LEGO barriers and sending pieces flying everywhere.

Nothing in the house that has a handle, lever, or tail has escaped his curiosity. He especially likes things that make a lot of noise—like piano keys and dropping dump trucks on tile floors. He wonders why you aren't more grateful for the knowledge he's given you: You know exactly how many toys the laundry hamper will hold, how to get Play-Doh out of a drain, and how much toothpaste a cat can eat before throwing up on the bed.

How might your stress level be reduced by understanding what's "normal" for a boy like Peter?

What steps could you take to maintain your sanity while letting your "boy be a boy"?

Elementary:
Pretend you're going to design a theme park for your son.

What would the theme be?

What kind of rides would it have? (For example, if your son is a thrill-seeker, he might like a loop-the-loop roller coaster; if he's into science, he might prefer a space shuttle that makes him weightless.)

Could any aspects of this theme park be worked into your son's real world? How? (For instance, does he need more room to run? Would he like to redecorate his room to reflect an interest in tigers? Could you and he make an "asteroid cruiser" out of cardboard boxes or a wagon with streamers?)

Adolescence:

Consider the following "risky behaviors." Which would you allow a teenager on a "boys will be boys" basis? Which would you ban? Which would you allow under certain conditions? Why?

	"Never!"	*"Yes…Under these conditions."*
dirt biking		
skydiving		
rock climbing		
kick boxing		
bungee jumping		
party hopping		
Internet surfing		
nose piercing		
drag racing		
prank calling		
smoking		
target shooting		

Try It:

Want to show your son that you appreciate the "boyishness" God gave him? Try celebrating "Male Appreciation Week" in your home. Here are some suggestions to get you started.

Preschool:
Many boys love to take things apart to see how they work. If your son is like this, you've probably already encountered him "fixing" things. You can turn this into an opportunity to affirm his masculinity by finding him something interesting to "fix" together.

Maybe you have an old clock or broken household appliance that could be sacrificed. Don't worry about whether you can actually fix it (or even get all the pieces back in). The point is to encourage your son in his natural inclination.

As you dismantle the item, you might ask him why he enjoys this, or how he thinks the inventor invented the machine. Listen carefully to what he says and show him you're proud of him by letting him keep the finished product as his "experiment." But don't forget to tell him to ask before he tries to fix anything else!

Elementary:
Here's a "dating game"—a time for your son to "go out with" Mom. The point: to learn how a man should treat a lady.

The setting for this date might be a favorite restaurant, miniature golf course, or simply a neighbor's house. Let your son pick the place, call to invite his date, and choose his outfit. You might even come up with a way for him to earn money to pay for the event.

Prepare your son by telling him that he "wins the game" if his date has a nice time. You may want to give him some rules. Examples might include:

• Ladies go first when entering rooms, ordering dinner, etc.

• It's polite to open doors for her.

• When at a table or getting into a car, make sure she's seated before you are.

• When walking on the sidewalk, protect her by staying on the street side.

You might also want to practice things to say during the date—not to mention table manners.

Adolescence:
Are there any nondangerous "risk-taking behaviors" your teen enjoys that you might be able to affirm this week?

Here are a few examples:

• Give him $10 and challenge him to invest it in some way, with the goal of doubling it in two weeks.

• If he's into public speaking, debate, or drama, congratulate him for having the courage to get up in front of people. If he's scheduled to do any of these things in a speech tournament or play, be sure to attend.

• Ask him to teach you how to use in-line skates or conquer a climbing wall.

• If he likes driving, let him chauffeur the family to a restaurant or church.

Single-Parent Tip:

If you're a single mom who doesn't feel confident about taking apart household appliances, try building something with your boy instead. It might be a puzzle, a tower of blocks, or the surface of an imaginary planet fashioned in clay.

If you're a single dad and want to try the "dating game," you may wish to enlist the help of an aunt or other relative, or a lady from church.

THE TROUBLE WITH BOYS

Quotes & Questions

"What is it about the masculine temperament that drives boys to tempt the laws of gravity and ignore the gentle voice of common sense—the one that says, 'Don't do it, Son'? Boys are like this because of the way they are wired neurologically and because of the influence of hormones that stimulate certain aggressive behavior.…You can't understand males of any age, including yourself or the one to whom you might be married, without knowing something about the forces that operate within."

—DR. JAMES DOBSON IN THE BOOK
BRINGING UP BOYS (TYNDALE HOUSE)

One old saying holds that boys are made of "snakes, snails, and puppy dog tails." What three things do you think boys are made of?

In your experience, how are boys and men alike? How are they different?

Video Journal

Use this space to take notes as you watch the video.

Boys are in a great deal of trouble today; they're more susceptible than girls are to…

At the foundation of the problem is…

The U.S. Census of 2001 showed…

This has a profound effect on boys because they…

To combat this, boys need…

Scriptures to Study

"The boys grew up, and Esau became a skillful hunter, a man of the open country, while Jacob was a quiet man, staying among the tents. Isaac, who had a taste for wild game, loved Esau, but Rebekah loved Jacob."

—GENESIS 25:27-28

"Sons are a heritage from the LORD,
children a reward from Him.
Like arrows in the hands of a warrior
are sons born in one's youth.
Blessed is the man
whose quiver is full of them.
They will not be put to shame
when they contend with their
enemies in the gate."

— PSALM 127:3-5

Apply It:

Testosterone, serotonin, and the amygdala influence male behavior in ways we may never fully understand. Testosterone accounts for a boy's aggressiveness and his tendency toward dominance and competition. Low serotonin levels can make a boy more volatile and impulsive. The brain structure called the amygdala, larger in males than females, responds to perceived threats in ways that can precipitate violence.

In the first two beakers are "normal" amounts of testosterone and serotonin. The third holds a "normal"-sized amygdala. Judging from your son's usual behavior, what would you guess are his hormone levels and amygdala size? Mark your answers on the first two beakers, and draw a new amygdala in the third.

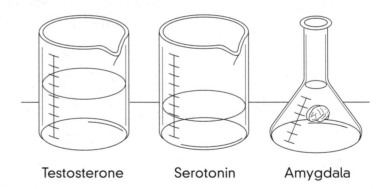

Testosterone   Serotonin   Amygdala

 **Try It:** *Looking to channel boy's "problem" tendencies in a constructive direction? Try these suggestions.*

Preschool:

Risk-taking: Encourage your son to meet a new person, try a new food, call a radio talk show (with your help), take a batch of cookies to a neighbor, or tell a friend about something he learned in church.

High energy: Have your son lead an "exercise workout" for the rest of the family, give the car or the dog a bath, or make "music" with a pots-and-pans marching band.

Elementary:

Competition: Stage contests to see who can set the table most quickly (without breaking anything), who can memorize the most Bible verses, who can give the most compliments in a day to other family members, who can stay quiet the longest, or who can rhyme the most times with "porcupine."

Boasting: Challenge your son to create a family newsletter touting the accomplishments of everyone in your household (including pets, if you have any); to write and perform a theme song about the greatest thing he's ever done (and how he felt); or to make a collage out of magazine pictures showing "Things I'll Do When I'm 20."

Adolescence:

Love of change: Ask your son to oil a squeaky hinge, paint a dreary room, level a wobbly table, or invent a new way to recycle junk mail or pop cans; challenge him to do a service project for someone less fortunate, or write a letter to the newspaper about a problem in your town.

Curiosity about sex: Listen together to a song that mentions love or sex and talk about it; read a book by Dr. James Dobson—*Preparing for Adolescence* (Regal Books) for younger teens, or *Life on the Edge* (Word) for older ones; interview a female friend of the family about the "top ten things girls wish guys knew"; read and discuss Bible passages like Genesis 2:24, Matthew 5:28, and Psalm 119:9–11.

W⚾UNDED
SPIRITS

Quotes & Questions

"Now, more than ever, boys are experiencing a crisis of confidence that reaches deep within the soul. Many of them are growing up believing they are unloved by their parents and are hated or disrespected by their peers. This results in a form of self-loathing that often serves as a prelude to violence, drug abuse, promiscuity, and suicide. It helps explain why both boys and girls do things that would otherwise make no sense, such as cutting their flesh, piercing sensitive body parts, tattooing themselves from head to toe, taking dangerous drugs, and/or identifying themselves with death, perversion, and satanic ritual. Some of them, it has been said, 'cry with bullets.'"

—DR. JAMES DOBSON IN THE BOOK
BRINGING UP BOYS (TYNDALE HOUSE)

How might the above quote help to explain the phenomenon of school shootings? What other causes of such incidents would you add?

How might a boy's crisis of confidence or self-hatred manifest itself in less dramatic ways?

Have you seen any of these symptoms in your son or a boy you know? If so, what have you done about it so far?

Video Journal

Use this space to take notes as you watch the video.

The "Wounded Spirits" syndrome is…

The syndrome is caused by…

Television and movies have worsened the problem by…

When boys are teased mercilessly, it can lead to…

To prevent "Wounded Spirits" syndrome, parents and other adults should…

Scriptures to Study

"Hear my prayer, O LORD;
let my cry for help come to You.
Do not hide Your face from me
when I am in distress.
Turn Your ear to me;
when I call, answer me quickly.
For my days vanish like smoke;
my bones burn like glowing embers.
My heart is blighted and withered like grass;
I forget to eat my food.
Because of my loud groaning
I am reduced to skin and bones.
I am like a desert owl,
like an owl among the ruins.
I lie awake; I have become
like a bird alone on a roof.
All day long my enemies taunt me;
those who rail against me use my name as a curse.
For I eat ashes as my food
and mingle my drink with tears
because of Your great wrath,
for You have taken me up and
thrown me aside.
My days are like the evening shadow;
I wither away like grass."

— PSALM 102:1–11

"Fathers, do not embitter your children, or they will become discouraged."

— COLOSSIANS 3:21

 Apply It:

Preschool:

Come up with some "spirit-wounding" and "spirit-preserving" ways in which a parent might respond to these situations.

1. While drawing pictures, your two-year-old boy has managed to decorate himself thoroughly with a washable purple marker. You tell him it's bath time. He yells his favorite word: "No!" You feel your blood pressure rising.

Spirit-wounding response:

Spirit-preserving response:

2. You pick up your four-year-old boy at preschool. As soon as you get to the car, he bursts into tears—something he does frequently, a "baby behavior" you wish he'd outgrow. This time he says a bigger boy grabbed his oatmeal cookie at lunch. What do you do?

Spirit-wounding response:

Spirit-preserving response:

Elementary:

Pretend you're on a committee assigned to come up with a school district "anti-bullying" policy.

What rules might you include?

What would teachers and administrators need to watch for?

What penalties would you assign for infractions?

Adolescence:

Rate the following events on a scale of 1 to 10, with 10 being the most damaging, according to their ability to wound a teenage boy's spirit. If you're doing this as a team, see whether you can reach consensus on your ratings.

____ Being dumped by the girl you dated exclusively for over a year.

____ Being unjustly accused of cheating after scoring the highest grade on a chemistry test.

____ Not making the football team, a goal you've had since fourth grade.

____ Having the nickname "Larry the Cucumber" due to the size of your nose.

____ Being scoffed at by the girl you've been trying to get to notice you.

____ Losing a class election by a landslide.

____ Being laughed at in the locker room because you don't want to shower with the other boys.

____ Flunking a history test when you were thinking about becoming a history professor.

____ Forgetting your lines in a school play in front of 800 staring people.

____ Overhearing your father call you a loser because you haven't been able to find a summer job.

____ Having your pants rip when you bend over to pick something up—in front of the whole class.

 Try It:

Has your son suffered a wound to his spirit? Go over this checklist of "wounded spirit" symptoms and see whether you recognize any in your boy. If so, follow through on the recommendation given.

Signs of depression in children:

___ Lethargy (not wanting to get out of bed in the morning, moping around the house, showing no interest in things that normally excite him)

___ Sleep disturbances

___ Stomach complaints

___ Open anger, hostility, rage (lashing out suddenly or unexpectedly at people or things)

What to do:

"If depression is a problem for your child, it is only symptomatic of something else that is bothering him or her. Help him or her verbalize feelings. Try to anticipate the explanation for sadness, and lead the youngster into conversations that provide an opportunity to ventilate. Make yourself available to listen, without judging or belittling the feelings expressed. Simply being understood is soothing for children and adults alike."

"If the symptoms are severe or if they last more than two weeks, I urge you to…seek professional help for your son. Prolonged depression can be destructive for human beings of any age and is especially dangerous to children."

—DR. JAMES DOBSON IN *THE COMPLETE MARRIAGE AND FAMILY HOME REFERENCE GUIDE* (TYNDALE HOUSE)

Signs of self-hatred or deep resentment in teens:

____ Overreactions to minor frustration

____ Fear of new social situations

____ Experimentation with drugs or alcohol

____ Difficulty sleeping or eating

____ Extreme isolation and withdrawal

____ Chewing the fingernails

____ Inability to make friends

____ Disinterest in school activities

____ Bullying others

____ Threatening suicide

What to do:

"Be especially vigilant when a child who has mentioned killing himself suddenly seems carefree and happy. That sometimes means he has decided to go through with the death wish and is no longer struggling with what has been bothering him. In each of these cases, I urge you to obtain professional help for those kids. Do not console yourself with the notion that 'he'll grow out of it.' That youngster may be in desperate need of assistance. Don't miss the opportunity to provide it."

—DR. JAMES DOBSON IN THE BOOK
BRINGING UP BOYS (TYNDALE HOUSE)

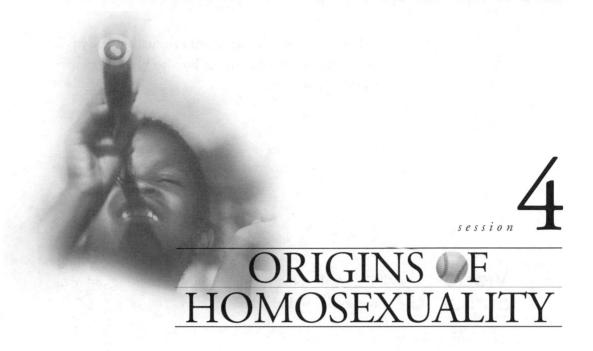

ORIGINS OF HOMOSEXUALITY

Quotes & Questions

"If homosexuality were genetically transmitted, it would be inevitable, immutable, irresistible, and untreatable. Fortunately, it is not. Prevention is effective. Change is possible. Hope is available. And Christ is in the business of healing."

—DR. JAMES DOBSON IN THE BOOK
BRINGING UP BOYS (TYNDALE HOUSE)

Do you agree with this statement? Why or why not?

What do you think causes homosexuality? Why is it important for the parents of boys to know the answer to this question?

Video Journal

Use this space to take notes as you watch the video.

The myth about homosexuality circulating today in the media and in schools is that...

Three facts that cast serious doubt on this theory are:

1.

2.

3.

The story of John Paulk shows…

The story of Mike Haley shows…

Scriptures to Study

"They exchanged the truth of God for a lie, and worshiped and served created things rather than the Creator—who is forever praised. Amen. Because of this, God gave them over to shameful lusts. Even their women exchanged natural relations for unnatural ones. In the same way the men also abandoned natural relations with women and were inflamed with lust for one another. Men committed indecent acts with other men, and received in themselves the due penalty for their perversion."

—ROMANS 1:25-27

 **Apply It:** What do you think the parents of these boys should do?

Case Study 1:

Aaron is three years old. Lately he's been asking his parents for a dollhouse like the one his friend Christina has. There are few boys in Aaron's neighborhood, and he plays almost exclusively with girls. When he does, he sometimes adopts a high-pitched voice that matches those of his playmates. Yesterday afternoon his mother found him trying on some of the necklaces she keeps on her dresser. "Now I'm a girl," he told her proudly. When his mother got him to give the jewelry back, he seemed "normal" again. *But for how long?* Mom wonders.

Case Study 2:

Tremaine is ten years old. His father always hoped for a son who would share his love of football, but Tremaine seems uninterested in sports of all kinds. The boy likes to spend time in the kitchen with his mother, learning to bake cakes and dice onions. He spends hours drawing pictures—and not pictures of superheroes, but of animals and sunsets. And he loves drama, relishing every chance to be in a play at school or church, reciting poems he's memorized, even singing along with characters in musicals he sees on TV. Tremaine is skinny and a bit uncoordinated, but doesn't exhibit any obviously effeminate mannerisms. His dad is worried that the boy won't grow up to be "a real man."

Case Study 3:

Kyle is fifteen. He's always been shy, finding it hard to make friends. Throughout elementary school he was teased about being slightly overweight and a "bookworm." During the last year, though, he's seemed to gain acceptance from several boys at school. At first Kyle's parents were glad to hear about these kids. But then they met the boys, most of whom seem effeminate. When Kyle's folks heard a rumor from other parents that the boys were "gay," they confronted Kyle. He bristled and said, "So what if they are? A person has to be himself."

 **Try It:** During the week, observe your son, then react to the following statements by circling your responses. If you have more than one boy, use a different-colored pencil to mark your responses for each.

1. I'm concerned that my son may be confused about his gender identity.

   AGREE   DISAGREE

2. I feel confident that my son is developing a normal masculine identity.

   AGREE   DISAGREE

3. It seems to me that my son displays effeminate mannerisms.

   AGREE   DISAGREE

4. I'm not sure I spend enough time affirming my son's masculinity.

   AGREE   DISAGREE

5. My son has stated that he thinks he's gay or bisexual.

   AGREE   DISAGREE

6. My son has said that he wishes he were a girl, or that he actually is a girl.

   AGREE   DISAGREE

7. My son has shown a preference for cross-dressing.

   AGREE   DISAGREE

8. My son needs more positive male role models.

   AGREE   DISAGREE

9. I probably need to talk with my son about gender identity, but don't know how.

   AGREE   DISAGREE

10. My son has a loving, respectful relationship with his father.

   AGREE   DISAGREE

PREVENTING HOMOSEXUALITY

Quotes & Questions

"Returning now to the issue of homosexuality, I am concerned not only about the sexual abuse of boys (and girls), but also about what they are being taught by the culture at large.…"

"Can you see how this pervasive teaching will be terribly confusing to very young boys who are experiencing a gender-identity crisis? How about the other cultural influences, including television and movies, that are urging boys and girls to 'think gay' and to experiment with role-reversal behavior? When combined with the absence or disengagement of fathers, we can begin to understand why the incidence of homosexuality appears to be rising and why more and more children and teens are reporting that they think they are homosexual."

—DR. JAMES DOBSON IN THE BOOK
BRINGING UP BOYS (TYNDALE HOUSE)

What do you think your son knows about homosexuality?

Where do you think he got this information?

How might the way you're raising him affect his gender identity? How do you feel about that?

Video Journal

Use this space to take notes as you watch the video.

According to psychologist and author Dr. Joseph Nicolosi, boys need special help to...

During the gender identity phase, boys need to detach from...

At the same time, they need to bond with…

Both parents should encourage their son to…

Parents, especially fathers, can help boys develop a healthy gender identity by…

Scriptures to Study

"Jesus continued: 'There was a man who had two sons. The younger one said to his father, "Father, give me my share of the estate." So he divided his property between them.

'Not long after that, the younger son got together all he had, set off for a distant country and there squandered his wealth in wild living. After he had spent everything, there was a severe famine in that whole country, and he began to be in need. So he went and hired himself out to a citizen of that country, who sent him to his fields to feed pigs. He longed to fill his stomach with the pods that the pigs were eating, but no one gave him anything.

'When he came to his senses, he said, "How many of my father's hired men have food to spare, and here I am starving to death! I will set out and go back to my father and say to him: Father, I have sinned against heaven and against you. I am no longer worthy to be called your son; make me like one of your hired men." So he got up and went to his father.

'But while he was still a long way off, his father saw him and was filled with compassion for him; he ran to his son, threw his arms around him and kissed him.

'The son said to him, "Father I have sinned against heaven and against you. I am no longer worthy to be called your son."

'But the father said to his servants, "Quick! Bring the best robe and put it on him. Put a ring on his finger and sandals on his feet. Bring the fattened calf and kill it. Let's have a feast and celebrate. For this son of mine was dead and is alive again; he was lost and is found." So they began to celebrate.

'Meanwhile, the older son was in the field. When he came near the house, he heard music and dancing. So he called one of the servants and asked him what was going on. "Your brother has come," he replied, "and your father has killed the fattened calf because he has him back safe and sound."

'The older brother became angry and refused to go in. So his father went out and pleaded with him. But he answered his father, "Look! All these years I've been slaving for you and never disobeyed your orders. Yet you never gave me even a young goat so I could celebrate with my friends. But when this son of yours who has squandered your property with prostitutes comes home, you kill the fattened calf for him!"

"'My son,' the father said, "you are always with me, and everything I have is yours. But we had to celebrate and be glad, because this brother of yours was dead and is alive again; he was lost and is found.'"

—LUKE 15:11-31

 Apply It:

"In 15 years, I have spoken with hundreds of homosexual men. I have never met one who said he had a loving, respectful relationship with his father."

—DR. JOSEPH NICOLOSI IN *PREVENTING HOMOSEXUALITY: A PARENT'S GUIDE*

Does the conclusion from the above quote match with your experience?

For fathers:

To help boys develop healthy masculine identities, fathers need to give their boys the three *A*'s: Affection, Attention, and Approval.

On a scale of 1 to 10 (10 being best), rate yourself and your own father in the following areas:

	YOU	YOUR FATHER
Showing son affection		
Giving son attention		
Showing son approval		

For married moms:

Try to come up with an example of something your husband has done (or could do) in each of the following areas:

Showing son affection

Giving son attention

Showing son approval

For single moms:

Indicate whether you think your son has a trustworthy male role model in his life to perform the following functions:

	YES	NO
Showing son affection		
Giving son attention		
Showing son approval		

 **Try It:**

For dads:

Showing AFFECTION to your son

In addition to expressing affection in words, try some of these:

- Hug
- Arm around the shoulders
- Handshake
- Pat on the knee
- Back scratch
- Pat on the back
- High-five
- Quick stroke of the hair
- Shoulder massage
- Wrestling
- Kiss on the cheek, forehead, or top of the head

Giving ATTENTION to your son

When you're listening to your son, avoid "multitasking." For example, don't try to read the paper or watch TV with one eye while he's telling you about his day.

Body language is important, too. Lean forward, making positive eye contact. Nod occasionally to show you're eager to hear what your son has to say. Slumping in your chair, folding your arms across your chest, or staring to one side of the speaker indicates you're not interested.

Showing APPROVAL to your son

Here are three ways to show approval:

1. Praise your son to someone else when he's around. Tell others what you like about your son—not just good grades or tennis skills, but also character traits.

2. Tuck a complimentary note into a lunch sack or binder—even a message as short as "I'm proud of you."

3. Catch him doing something right, and mention it. For example, "I noticed you showed mercy to your sister when you complimented her new haircut instead of making a joke about it." Or, "I saw you pick up the little boy down the street when he fell off his scooter. I can tell you care about people."

—Adapted from *Parents' Guide to the Spiritual Mentoring of Teens* (Tyndale House)

For single moms:
Finding a Male Role Model for Your Son

"To every single mom who is on this quest, let me emphasize first that you have an invaluable resource in our heavenly Father. He created your children and they are precious to Him. How do I know that? Because he said repeatedly in His Word that He has a special tenderness for fatherless children and their mothers. There are many references in Scripture to their plight [see Deuteronomy 10:17–18; 27:19; Psalm 68:5; Zechariah 7:10]."

"[The Lord] is waiting for you to ask Him for help. I have seen miraculous answers to prayer on behalf of those who have sought His help in what seemed like impossible situations."

"Make an all-out effort to find a father-substitute for your boys. An uncle or a neighbor or a coach or a musical director or a Sunday school teacher may do the trick. Placing your boys under the influence of such a man for even a single hour per week can make a great difference. Get them involved in Boy Scouts, Boy's Club, soccer, or Little League. Check out Big Brothers as a possibility. Give your boys biographies, and take them to movies or rent videos that focus on strong masculine (but moral) heroes. However you choose to solve the problem, do not let the years go by without a man's influence in the lives of your boys."

—DR. JAMES DOBSON IN THE BOOK
BRINGING UP BOYS (TYNDALE HOUSE)

session 6

R⚾UTINE PANIC

Quotes & Questions

"The trouble we are having with our children is linked directly to routine panic and the increasing isolation and detachment from you, their parents. Furthermore, boys typically suffer more from these conditions than do girls. Why? Because boys are more likely to get off-course when they are not guided and supervised carefully. They are inherently more volatile and less stable emotionally. They founder in chaotic, unsupervised, and undisciplined circumstances."

"Fifty-nine percent of today's kids come home to an empty house."

—Dr. James Dobson in the book
Bringing Up Boys (Tyndale House)

When you read this statement, how do you feel? Do you know why?

How would you describe the "busyness level" in your home?

How does it affect you? How might it affect the boy(s) in your home?

Video Journal

Use this space to take notes as you watch the video.

Boys need to learn four things about their possible future roles in the family:

1.

2.

3.

4.

"Routine panic" is…

The effects of routine panic on children include…

Boys especially need time with parents because…

To find more time with their kids, parents
should consider…

Scriptures to Study

"As Jesus and His disciples were on their way, He came to a village where a woman named Martha opened her home to Him. She had a sister called Mary, who sat at the Lord's feet listening to what He said. But Martha was distracted by all the preparations that had to be made. She came to Him and asked, 'Lord, don't You care that my sister has left me to do the work by myself? Tell her to help me!'

"'Martha, Martha,' the Lord answered, 'you are worried and upset about many things, but only one thing is needed. Mary has chosen what is better, and it will not be taken away from her.'"

—Luke 10:38–42

 Apply It: With which of the following quotes, taken from Dr. Dobson's book *Bringing Up Boys*, do you most identify? Why?

QUOTE 1

"Americans...are already the most vacation-starved people in the industrialized world, with an average of thirteen vacation days per year, compared with twenty-five or more in Japan, Canada, Britain, Germany, and Italy. The study revealed that 32 percent of those surveyed said they work and eat lunch at the same time, and another 32 percent said they never leave the building once they arrive at work. Some 34 percent said they have such pressing jobs that they have no breaks or downtime while on the job. Nineteen percent say their job makes them feel older than they are, and 17 percent say work causes them to lose sleep at night. Seventeen percent said it is difficult to take time off or leave work even in an emergency, and 8 percent said they believe if they were to become seriously ill, they would be fired or demoted." (*Business Wire,* February 21, 2001)

QUOTE 2

"It is becoming less common these days for a teenager to have time isolated for focused interaction with family members. Most of the time they spend with their family is what you might call 'family and time': family and TV, family and dinner, family and homework, etc. The lives of each family member are usually so jam-packed that the opportunity to spend time together doing unique activities—talking about life, visiting special places, playing games, and sharing spiritual explorations—has to be scheduled in advance. Few do so." (George Barna, *Generation Next* [Regal Books, 1995])

QUOTE 3

"According to a recent survey by Youth Intelligence, a market research and trend-tracking firm in New York, 68 percent of 3,000 married and single young women said they'd ditch work if they could afford to. And a Cosmo poll of 800 women revealed the same startling statistic: two out of three respondents would rather kick back *a casa* than climb the corporate ladder. 'It's no fleeting fantasy—these women honestly aspire to the domestic life, and many will follow through with it,' says Jane Buckingham, president of Youth Intelligence." (Judy Dutton, "Meet the New Housewife Wanna-bes," *Cosmopolitan,* June 2000)

Try It:

This week, try keeping track of the quantity and quality of time you spend with your boy(s). You may be surprised at the results. If you're caring for more than one boy, make a copy of this sheet for each one.

	Quantity of time spent	Quality of time spent (Describe what you did and the effect you think it had on the boy)
Sunday		
Monday		
Tuesday		
Wednesday		
Thursday		
Friday		
Saturday		

QUESTIONS FROM PARENTS & GRANDPARENTS

Quotes & Questions

"Before you know it, that child at your feet will become a young man who will pack his bags and take his first halting steps into the adult world. Then it will be your turn. By all expectations, you should have decades of health and vigor left to invest in whatever God calls you to do. But for now, there is a higher calling. I feel obligated to tell you this, whether my words are popular or not. Raising children who have been loaned to us for a brief moment outranks every other responsibility. Besides, living by that priority when kids are small will produce the greatest rewards at maturity."

—Dr. James Dobson in the book
Bringing Up Boys (Tyndale House)

Do you think your parents spent enough time with you when you were a child? Why or why not?

When was the last time you truly enjoyed spending time with your boy(s)? What would it take to repeat that experience?

Video Journal

Use this space to take notes as you watch the video.

One question with which I identified was...

One answer I found helpful was...

One piece of advice I could have given is...

Scriptures to Study

"Then Jesus said to His disciples: 'Therefore I tell you, do not worry about your life, what you will eat; or about your body, what you will wear. Life is more than food, and the body more than clothes. Consider the ravens: They do not sow or reap, they have no storeroom or barn; yet God feeds them. And how much more valuable you are than birds! Who of you by worrying can add a single hour to his life? Since you cannot do this very little thing, why do you worry about the rest?

"'Consider how the lilies grow. They do not labor or spin. Yet I tell you, not even Solomon in all his splendor was dressed like one of these. If that is how God clothes the grass of the field, which is here today, and tomorrow is thrown into the fire, how much more will He clothe you, O you of little faith! And do not set your heart on what you will eat or drink; do not worry about it. For the pagan world runs after such things, and your Father knows that you need them. But seek His kingdom, and these things will be given to you as well.'"

—Luke 12:22–31

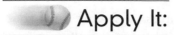 **Apply It:** Which of the following changes might make your lifestyle less hectic—and give you more time to parent? Circle your responses.

1. Watching less TV.

• This would help, and I can start this week.

• This would help, but I'll need time to work out the details.

• This would help, but there's no way it can happen.

• This probably wouldn't help even if I did it.

2. Going from a two-income household to one income.

• This would help, and I can start this week.

• This would help, but I'll need time to work out the details.

• This would help, but there's no way it can happen.

• This probably wouldn't help even if I did it.

3. Working at home.

• This would help, and I can start this week.

• This would help, but I'll need time to work out the details.

• This would help, but there's no way it can happen.

• This probably wouldn't help even if I did it.

4. Spending less time on hobbies or recreation.

• This would help, and I can start this week.

• This would help, but I'll need time to work out the details.

• This would help, but there's no way it can happen.

• This probably wouldn't help even if I did it.

5. Getting a slower wristwatch.

- This would help, and I can start this week.
- This would help, but I'll need time to work out the details.
- This would help, but there's no way it can happen.
- This probably wouldn't help even if I did it.

6. Getting a job with a shorter commute.

- This would help, and I can start this week.
- This would help, but I'll need time to work out the details.
- This would help, but there's no way it can happen.
- This probably wouldn't help even if I did it.

7. Postponing a goal (getting a degree, remodeling the house, etc.).

- This would help, and I can start this week.
- This would help, but I'll need time to work out the details.
- This would help, but there's no way it can happen.
- This probably wouldn't help even if I did it.

8. Getting rid of some possessions so I don't have to spend time maintaining them.

- This would help, and I can start this week.
- This would help, but I'll need time to work out the details.
- This would help, but there's no way it can happen.
- This probably wouldn't help even if I did it.

9. Reducing my work hours.

- This would help, and I can start this week.

- This would help, but I'll need time to work out the details.

- This would help, but there's no way it can happen.

- This probably wouldn't help even if I did it.

10. Better managing the time I do have.

- This would help, and I can start this week.

- This would help, but I'll need time to work out the details.

- This would help, but there's no way it can happen.

- This probably wouldn't help even if I did it.

 Try It:

This week, try setting aside a short "sabbath" time each day to spend one-on-one with your son. Use the following ideas to get you thinking about refreshing, renewing things to do together.

Preschool:

Sunday: Hide pennies around your home and have a treasure hunt.

Monday: Play "volleyballoon" by batting a balloon back and forth over a net made of tied-together plastic bags.

Tuesday: Make snakes with modeling clay or dough.

Wednesday: Sit in a darkened room, listen carefully, and see how many separate sounds you can identify.

Thursday: Cut out pictures from old magazines to give you ideas of things to pray about.

Friday: Build a fort out of blankets and chairs and take a nap in it.

Saturday: Have a "pretend picnic" on a blanket on the floor.

Elementary:

Sunday: Make pizza or ice cream sundaes and let your son choose the toppings.

Monday: Get two books of jokes or riddles from the library and take turns reading them to each other.

Tuesday: Make up obstacle courses and time each other as you navigate them. This can be done outdoors (run to the tree, hop on one foot to the fence, then come back and give me five) or indoors (touch that wall, get a napkin from the kitchen, and return while flapping your arms and reciting the alphabet backward).

Wednesday: Tell each other how your day might have been different if you could have seen Jesus with you wherever you went.

Thursday: Turn cupcakes into spiders by adding legs made of pipe cleaners or toothpicks.

Friday: Play a favorite board game, but let your son change the rules.

Saturday: Try using the wrong equipment for a sport. For example, use a tennis ball to shoot baskets, or a table tennis paddle and beanbag to play baseball.

Adolescence:

Sunday: Rent a video of an old movie that looks especially dull. Watch it together with the sound off, making up dialogue as you go.

Monday: Play "Can you top this?" with the weirdest, most embarrassing, most frustrating, most boring, and funniest events of your day.

Tuesday: Look over the calendar for the next month and draw a star on each day that either of you might be under more stress than usual. Plan to pray for each other on those days.

Wednesday: Ask your son to help you memorize a passage of Scripture, using any method he thinks will work.

Thursday: Go through your home and take turns snapping photos of the things you consider most valuable. Be sure to take pictures of each other before you're finished.

Friday: Ask your son's advice about a problem you face at work, or his opinion about a change you'd like to make in your household routine.

Saturday: Go to the market together and let your son pick out the food and beverage for supper. The catch: Everything has to be the same color.

MEN 'R' FOOLS

Quotes & Questions

"[The] war between the sexes is extremely important for parents to understand, because it influences the way they raise their children. Feminist Karla Mantilla summarized the philosophy behind it in an article entitled 'Kids Need "Fathers" Like Fish Need Bicycles.' She wrote, 'I submit that men tend to emphasize values such as discipline, power, control, stoicism, and independence. Sure, there can be some good from these things, but they are mostly damaging to kids (and other living things). They certainly made my son suffer an isolated and tortured existence until he began to see that there was a way out of the trap of masculinity.'

"The trap of masculinity? That is the way many feminists view maleness. A centerpiece of this hostility is seen in an ongoing effort to convince us that 'Men are fools.' It claims that the majority of males are immature, impulsive, selfish, weak, and not very bright. Evidence of that campaign can still be observed in almost every dimension of the culture."

—DR. JAMES DOBSON IN THE BOOK
BRINGING UP BOYS (TYNDALE HOUSE)

What kinds of experiences do you suppose might have shaped Karla Mantilla's opinions about males?

Have you seen evidence that opinions like hers still shape our culture? If so, what is it?

Video Journal

Use this space to take notes as you watch the video.

Feminism in the 1960s was characterized by...

Feminism today is different in some ways, but...

It has become politically correct to view men as...

This can affect boys because…

TV commercials illustrate this bias by…

Scriptures to Study

"So God created man in His own image, in the image of God He created him; male and female He created them."

"God saw all that He had made, and it was very good. And there was evening, and there was morning—the sixth day."

—Genesis 1:27, 31

"Deacons, likewise, are to be men worthy of respect, sincere, not indulging in much wine, and not pursuing dishonest gain. They must keep hold of the deep truths of the faith with a clear conscience. They must first be tested; and then if there is nothing against them, let them serve as deacons.

"In the same way, their wives are to be women worthy of respect, not malicious talkers but temperate and trustworthy in everything."

"Do not rebuke an older man harshly, but exhort him as if he were your father. Treat younger men as brothers, older women as mothers, and younger women as sisters, with absolute purity."

—1 TIMOTHY 3:8–11; 5:1–2

 **Apply It:** Compare and contrast the following TV husbands and wives. Who's smarter? Who's more mature? Who's out of control? If you aren't familiar with all the shows, try to come up with other examples.

The Simpsons: Homer vs. Marge

The King of Queens: Doug vs. Carrie

Everybody Loves Raymond: Ray vs. Debra

The Cosby Show: Cliff vs. Clair

Dharma and Greg: Greg vs. Dharma

The Munsters: Herman vs. Lily

King of the Hill: Hank vs. Peggy

The Addams Family: Gomez vs. Morticia

I Love Lucy: Ricky vs. Lucy

Leave It to Beaver: Ward vs. June

 **Try It:**

Preschool:

Look together through the comics pages of the newspaper. Have your son draw a circle around each boy and man portrayed. Ask: Is this guy smart or silly? How is he like a real-life boy or man? How is he different? Do the boys and men in the comics seem dumber than the girls and ladies? Assure your son that even if the comics tend to make fun of "dopey" dads and "rude" boys, and even if girls and ladies in the comics are often the "wise" and "normal" ones, there's nothing wrong with being a real-life boy.

Elementary:

View a few TV sitcoms, cartoons, or commercials together (if you're not sure they'll be appropriate, tape them in advance and pre-screen them). Have your son watch for the ways in which boys and men are portrayed, especially compared to the depiction of female characters. Is it true that male characters are much more likely to be clueless, sloppy, insensitive, dim-witted, crude, and selfish? How does your son feel about that? Explain that no matter how guys are depicted on TV, there's no reason to be embarrassed about being one—and that we can find much better male role models in places like the Bible.

Adolescence:

Choose a man you admire, perhaps a nearby relative or a friend from church, and arrange to have lunch with him and your son. During the conversation, point out some of the qualities you admire in this man. Ask him to explain who some of *his* male role models were. Don't turn the lunch into a lecture; just let the man be an example to your son of what a male can and should be.

BOYS 'R' FOOLS TOO

"Please understand that I have nothing but respect and admiration for girls and women. I have been happily married to the 'love of my life' for more than forty years and have articulated the needs and concerns of women in several of my previous books. Nevertheless, I have to call it as I see it. And as I see it, boys are desperately in need of friends.

"They are the victims of a long and costly battle between the sexes that has vilified the essence of masculinity and ripped into the world of children. And that is not good. Pitting boys and girls against each other as competitors and enemies cannot be healthy for anyone!"

—DR. JAMES DOBSON IN THE BOOK
BRINGING UP BOYS (TYNDALE HOUSE)

How has the "war between the sexes" affected your son(s)?

Which of the following does your son need more: to respect himself, or to respect the opposite sex? How do you know?

Video Journal

Use this space to take notes as you watch the video.

Men are disrespected not only in TV commercials but also...

An example of this is...

This attitude toward men leaves boys…

Conventional wisdom says that girls are…

Boys need extra help in school because…

Scriptures to Study

"However, each one of you also must love his wife as he loves himself, and the wife must respect her husband."

—EPHESIANS 5:33

"Husbands, in the same way be considerate as you live with your wives, and treat them with respect as the weaker partner and as heirs with you of the gracious gift of life, so that nothing will hinder your prayers."

—1 PETER 3:7

Apply It: If you speak disparagingly of the opposite sex, or if you refer to females as sex objects, those attitudes will translate directly into dating and marital relationships later on. Remember that your goal is to prepare a boy to lead a family when he's grown and to show him how to earn the respect of those he serves.

1. Tell him it is great to laugh and have fun with his friends, but advise him not to be "goofy." Guys who are goofy are not respected, and people, especially girls and women, do not follow boys and men whom they disrespect.

___ I've taught this principle.

___ I don't agree with this principle.

___ I hope to teach this principle.

___ I agree with this principle,
      but don't think I could teach it.

2. Also, tell your son that he is never to hit a girl under any circumstances. Remind him that she is not as strong as he is and that she is deserving of his respect.

___ I've taught this principle.

___ I don't agree with this principle.

___ I hope to teach this principle.

___ I agree with this principle,
      but don't think I could teach it.

3. Not only should he not hurt her, but he should protect her if she is threatened. When he is strolling along with a girl on the street, he should walk on the outside, nearer the cars. That is symbolic of his responsibility to take care of her.

____ I've taught this principle.

____ I don't agree with this principle.

____ I hope to teach this principle.

____ I agree with this principle,
    but don't think I could teach it.

4. When he is on a date, he should pay for her food and entertainment. Also (and this is simply my opinion), girls should not call boys on the telephone—at least not until a committed relationship has developed. Guys must be the initiators, planning the dates and asking for the girl's company. Teach your son to open doors for girls and to help them with their coats or their chairs in a restaurant. When a guy goes to her house to pick up his date, tell him to get out of the car and knock on the door. Never honk. Teach him to stand, in formal situations, when a woman leaves the room or a table, or when she returns. This is a way of showing respect for her. If he treats her like a lady, she will treat him like a man. It's a great plan.

____ I've taught these principles.

____ I don't agree with these principles.

____ I hope to teach these principles.

____ I agree with these principles,
    but don't think I could teach them.

5. Remind your sons repeatedly and emphatically of the biblical teaching about sexual immorality—and why someone who violates those laws not only hurts himself, but also wounds the girl and cheats the man she will eventually marry. Tell them not to take anything that doesn't belong to them—especially the moral purity of a woman.

_____ I've taught this principle.

_____ I don't agree with this principle.

_____ I hope to teach this principle.

_____ I agree with this principle,
          but don't think I could teach it.

"Some of the ideas I've suggested sound like 'yesterday.' But they still make sense to me because most of them are biblically based. They also contribute to harmonious relationships between the sexes, which will pay dividends for those who will marry. Dr. Michael Gurian said it best: 'Every time you raise a loving, wise, and responsible man, you have created a better world for women.'"

(ADAPTED FROM THE BOOK *BRINGING UP BOYS* BY DR. JAMES DOBSON [TYNDALE HOUSE])

 Try It:

How can you teach boys to respect themselves as males, and to respect and protect females? Here are some ideas.

Preschool:
Self-respect. Sit down with your boy and a family photo album (or some home videos). Look together at pictures of male relatives, pointing out their positive traits. Tell

your boy about some of the same traits he's displayed—or how he might grow up to be like some of the men. Example: "There's Uncle Ray. He's always been good at fixing cars. You have some Hot Wheels cars, don't you? Maybe you'll be like Uncle Ray someday."

Respect for the opposite sex. If your boy has a sister, enlist his aid next time she cleans her room. Help him to be careful with her toys and other items, showing respect for her by showing respect for her special possessions. If he has no sister, try practicing holding the door open for girls and ladies next time you go to church or the mall.

Protecting the opposite sex. Play an imagination game involving your son and Mom or an older sister. Pretend that a semi-darkened room in your home is a "scary cave" with snakes or other hazards on the floor. Give your son a flashlight and tell him that he's the "brave explorer" who must lead Mom or Sister through the cave. Mom or Sister should follow his lead, expressing plenty of gratitude for his courage.

Elementary:

Self-respect. Each week for a month, stage an awards ceremony for the boy or boys in your household. Give out homemade or purchased medals or certificates commending positive, masculine qualities you've observed. Examples: taking the initiative to right a wrong, showing strength in the face of peer pressure, faithfully providing food for a pet.

Respect for the opposite sex. Many boys in this age group are known for an "I hate girls" attitude. Have your son choose a girl at school or in the neighborhood and encourage him to make a list of the girl's positive traits. To get him thinking, ask questions like, "Have you ever seen her help someone? Does she smile or tell jokes? Is she polite to the teacher? Does she seem to know much about music or geography or baseball?"

Protecting the opposite sex. Ask your boy, "What could you do if you saw a bully threatening a girl at school?" Brainstorm possibilities, from alerting a teacher to physically intervening. Role-play what the boy could do and say in a such a situation.

Adolescence:

Self-respect. Buy your son a new men's wallet. Put a copy of your favorite picture of him in it, and tell him why it's your favorite. If possible, put a copy of the same picture in your wallet, too, and let him know that you'll be showing it to others when the opportunity arises.

Respect for the opposite sex. If your teen is dating, loan him a camera next time he goes out. Offer to pay for the date if he gets a bystander to take the following photos during the date: a shot of himself opening a door for the girl; a picture of himself helping the girl with her coat; a photo of himself helping the girl with her chair in a restaurant; a picture of the two of them on the side-walk, with the boy on the street side.

Protecting the opposite sex. Find an appropriate magazine, newspaper, or Internet article about the problem of battered wives or violence against women. Read it, and invite your teen to read it. Discuss it, asking questions like these: "What do you think about a man who acts this way? What attitude do you suppose he has toward women? How do you think God wants a man to deal with anger? If you knew a girl at school was being abused by her boyfriend, what would you do?"

QUESTIONS FROM PARENTS & GRANDPARENTS

Quotes & Questions

"Boys need structure, they need supervision, and they need to be civilized. When raised in a laissez-faire environment that is devoid of leadership, they often begin to challenge social conventions and common sense. Many often crash and burn during the adolescent years. Some never fully recover.

"We received a letter at Focus on the Family…from a mother who has observed the same trends that concern me. She wrote, 'What has become of the backbone of parents today?'

"This mom is absolutely right. Parents are obligated to take charge of their young sons and teach them respectful and responsible behavior. When they fail in that mission, trouble stalks both generations."

—DR. JAMES DOBSON IN THE BOOK
BRINGING UP BOYS (TYNDALE HOUSE)

If you could ask Dr. Dobson one question about raising boys, what would it be?

Do you think the answer to your question would have more to do with love or discipline? Why?

Video Journal

Use this space to take notes as you watch the video.

One question with which I identified was…

One answer I found helpful was…

One piece of advice I could have given is…

Scriptures to Study

"Train a child in the way he should go, and when he is old he will not turn from it."

—PROVERBS 22:6

"As soon as Jesus was baptized, He went up out of the water. At that moment heaven was opened, and He saw the Spirit of God descending like a dove and lighting on Him. And a voice from heaven said, 'This is My Son, whom I love; with Him I am well pleased.'"

—MATTHEW 3:16-17

 Apply It:

One way to stay close is to connect through a boy's natural interests. As a first step, think of a boy. Come up with two or three of his favorite activities and write them in the space below.

Now choose one of those activities—one you could spend some time doing together—and write it here.

Next, think of an area in which this boy needs guidance. (Examples: table manners, prayer, being more organized about homework, choosing a career.) Write it below.

Now try to think of a parallel between the activity you chose and the guidance the boy needs. For instance, playing basketball takes teamwork; so does getting chores done in a family. Building a baking-soda-and-vinegar volcano requires doing things in the right order; so does getting homework finished. How could you point out that parallel in your own words, without being preachy or negative? Write what you might say.

 **Try It:**

Staying close takes persistence and creativity. Consider some of the following ideas for providing the loving guidance your boy needs.

Preschool:

To teach good behavior, make a "Behavior Calendar." Choose a goal you'd like to see the boy reach. (Examples: to tell the truth about whether he brushed his teeth before bed; to take one more bath per week; to stop pulling the cat's tail.) Make a calendar showing positive and negative repercussions that will occur when the boy achieves or fails to achieve the goal that day or week. For instance, if the goal is "no lying," a daily reward could be an extra story read at bedtime; a penalty might be a "time out."

In addition to daily steps, you may want to offer a bigger prize (a certificate, small trophy, or toy) at the end of the week or month.

Elementary:

Instead of asking the generic, "What happened at school today?" and getting a vague response, ask questions like these:

1. If I could have listened to your thoughts during recess today, what would I have heard?

2. Who had the best lunch at your table? Who had the worst?

3. What animal did your teacher most resemble today? Why? What animal were you most like?

4. If you'd been the principal of your school today, what would have been different?

5. What do you deserve a reward for doing at school today?

Adolescence:

Does your teen's social whirl make it tough to stay close?

1. If he doesn't have a cell phone, consider getting or loaning him one when he goes out. It can be a good way for him to let you know where he is, what he's doing, and when something unexpected comes up.

2. Talk in *advance* about what he'll do if alcohol or other drugs appear at an event he's attending. Explain that if he calls, you'll come and get him.

3. Sit down at the beginning of each month and mark your commitments on a calendar. Work out schedule conflicts before they happen.

THE ULTIMATE PRIORITY

Quotes & Questions

"Parents…need to 'play offense'—to capitalize on the impressionable years of childhood by instilling in their sons the antecedents of character. Their assignment during two brief decades will be to transform their boys from immature and flighty youngsters into honest, caring men who will be respectful of women, loyal and faithful in marriage, keepers of commitments, strong and decisive leaders, good workers, and secure in their masculinity. And of course, the ultimate goal for people of faith is to give each child an understanding of Scripture and a lifelong passion for Jesus Christ."

—DR. JAMES DOBSON IN THE BOOK
BRINGING UP BOYS (TYNDALE HOUSE)

How would you prioritize the goals listed in the above quote?

For your son, how would you compare his "spiritual age" (understanding of and commitment to God) with his chronological age? (For example, is he twelve years old but still a spiritual infant?) How do you feel about his spiritual age?

Video Journal

Use this space to take notes as you watch the video.

The tug-of-war for the hearts and minds of children is about…

Protecting children is up to…

Parents need to balance…

Bridges must be built between parents and
children before...

The ultimate priority is to...

The window of opportunity for this to happen
tends to be...

Scriptures to Study

"These commandments that I give you today are to be
upon your hearts. Impress them on your children.
Talk about them when you sit at home and when you
walk along the road, when you lie down and when
you get up. Tie them as symbols on your hands and
bind them on your foreheads. Write them on the
doorframes of your houses and on your gates."

—DEUTERONOMY 6:6–9

"My son, do not forget my teaching,
  but keep my commands in your heart,
  for they will prolong your life many years
  and bring you prosperity.
  Let love and faithfulness never leave you;
  bind them around your neck,
  write them on the tablet of your heart.
  Then you will win favor and a good name
  in the sight of God and man.
  Trust in the LORD with all your heart
  and lean not on your own understanding;
  in all your ways acknowledge Him,
  and He will make your paths straight."

—PROVERBS 3:1–6

 Apply It:

Underline the statements you think your son could make at this point in his life. Draw a box around those you think he couldn't truthfully make now, but that you'd like him to be able to make someday.

"I pray on my own about things that matter to me."
"Church is boring."
"I have a personal relationship with Jesus."
"God made the world."
"Christians are hypocrites."
"I read the Bible on my own regularly."
"Jesus loves me."
"I do things to help people who have less than I do."
"I want to follow Jesus."
"I don't get anything out of Sunday school."
"I like going to church."

"I understand most of what I read in the Bible."
"Religion isn't a 'guy thing.'"
"My faith makes a difference in my decisions."

 **Try It:** Have some family fun—and teach a spiritual principle at the same time. Here are heritage-building ideas adapted from *The Focus on the Family Parents' Guide to the Spiritual Growth of Children* (Tyndale House).

Preschool:

• Make tunnels and tents throughout the house with blankets, card tables, chairs, boxes, and whatever you can find. These are especially great during thunderstorms when you're armed with a flashlight and a big bowl of popcorn to eat. Read Psalm 91 and talk about how God covers us with His love.

• Throw a birthday party for a pet and invite all the neighbor kids. For a dog party, serve children "dog kibble" (Cocoa Puffs); for a cat, serve goldfish crackers; for a bird, serve sunflower seeds. Show how all God's creation is special and worth celebrating.

Elementary:

• Walk on the ceiling with mirrors. For this, you take a hand mirror and hold it about waist height. Look down into it and you will see the ceiling. Begin to walk through the house. Step over any obstacle you see in the mirror. This works best in homes with lots of doorways and ceiling beams. Walking down stairs is a real challenge! Your family can learn that basing your life on man's ideas is much like walking "on the ceiling," while walking in the truth is like seeing life as it really is.

- Make hats out of paper plates and wild and silly objects: toys, dry food, crafts—the more outrageous the better. Everyone must wear his or her hat to dinner and tell a story about the hat. Go to McDonald's or out for ice cream wearing the hats. Pretend to be very serious while people stare at you. Remind your family that everyone is to be prepared to share about the hope that is within them. Their relationship with Jesus makes them "different," and sometimes people might wonder about it.

Adolescence:
- Have a cooperation dinner—everyone must feed the person to his or her left. As Christians, we are to encourage and help one another.

- Make a video called "Arms." This takes two performers. One person stands in front of a table with items on it, like a phone, a bowl of applesauce or cereal, and a pen and piece of paper. This person clasps his hands behind his back. A second person hides behind him and puts his arms through the sleeves of the person in front of him. Now have the standing person speak and tell the story, or say things that involve the items on the table. The "arms" must pick up the phone and hold it to the person's ear, feed him, make hand motions as if he is the person speaking, and so on. Use this to illustrate the idea of not letting ourselves be manipulated by peer pressure into doing things we wouldn't do on our own.

Note: For more on teaching your children spiritual values, visit the FaithLaunch Website at www.focusonyourchild.com/faith/faithlaunch

session 12

TAKING ACTION

Quotes & Questions

"Prayer is the key to everything. I'm reminded of a story told by a rookie player for the Chicago Bulls in the National Basketball Association. One night, the incomparable Michael Jordan scored sixty-eight points, and the rookie was sent in for the last couple of minutes of the game. When the young man was interviewed by a reporter afterwards, he said, 'Yeah, it was a great night. Michael Jordan and I scored sixty-eight points.' That's the way I feel about parenting and prayer. We do all we can to score a few points, but the greater contribution is made by the creator of children."

—DR. JAMES DOBSON IN THE BOOK
BRINGING UP BOYS (TYNDALE HOUSE)

Of all the principles discussed in this course, which one do you think you'll need the most supernatural help to apply? Why?

In the space below, try writing a prayer of thanks for what God has done so far in your son's life—or a prayer asking for His help in a specific area of boy-raising.

Scriptures to Study

"I can do everything through Him who gives me strength."

—PHILIPPIANS 4:13

"Look to the LORD and His strength; seek His face always."

—1 CHRONICLES 16:11

"Plans fail for lack of counsel, but with many advisers they succeed."

—PROVERBS 15:22

"Commit to the LORD whatever you do, and your plans will succeed."

—PROVERBS 16:3

"In the same way, faith by itself, if it is not accompanied by action, is dead."

—JAMES 2:17

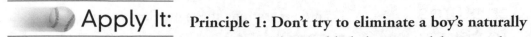 Apply It:

Principle 1: Don't try to eliminate a boy's naturally aggressive and excitable behavior; celebrate and shape and civilize it.

____ I need to lighten up about "typical boy" activity that's been irritating me.

____ My son needs more civilizing.

____ I need to let my son know that I love him the way he is.

Principle 2: To prevent the "Wounded Spirit" syndrome in a boy, deal decisively with bullies, reduce exposure to violence, and watch for signs of depression.

____ My son faces bullying, and I need to resolve it.

____ My son sees or hears too much violent entertainment, and I need to intervene.

____ I'm concerned that my son may be depressed.

Principle 3: Stay close to your son, both emotionally and as a vigilant guide; convey rules in the context of a loving relationship.

____ I need to be clearer about what the rules are in our home.

____ I do okay as a rule-giver, but I'm afraid the relationship isn't what it should be.

____ I fear I'm losing track of my son and what he's doing.

Principle 4: To help your son develop a healthy gender identity, make sure he receives appropriate affection, attention, and approval from his father (or, in the father's absence, a trustworthy male role model).

____ I have a hard time showing my son affection.

____ My boy hears more criticism than approval from me.

____ I need to find a good male role model for my son.

Principle 5: Spend both quantity and quality time with your son, even if it means changing your lifestyle to make that time available.

____ I'm not spending enough time with my son.

____ We spend time together, but I don't think he gets much out of it.

____ I'm so busy that my life is out of control.

Principle 6: Counteract the effects of male-bashing in our culture by affirming your son's masculinity and his value as a person.

____ I need to talk with my son about antimale messages he sees on TV or in the movies.

____ My son's education is suffering because of antimale bias in the school system.

____ My son needs to learn more respect for himself and for the opposite sex.

Principle 7: Make your son's relationship with God the first priority as you raise him.

____ I need to take better advantage of "teachable moments" with my son.

____ I fear negative experiences at church or at home may be decreasing my son's interest in God.

____ I need to be more intentional about encouraging my son to accept Jesus as Savior.

Try It:

1. Dealing with boyishness

____ I need to lighten up about "typical boy" activity that's been irritating me.

Action: Next time my son is rambunctious (without being disobedient), I'll respond by…

____ My son needs more civilizing.

Action: This week I will begin to teach this boy that "good manners" include…

____ I need to let my son know that I love him the way he is.

Action: During the next 24 hours, I will tell this boy…

2. Preventing "Wounded Spirit" syndrome

____ My son faces bullying, and I need to resolve it.

Action: This week I will speak to the bully's parents or school authorities, and tell them…

____ My son sees or hears too much violent entertainment, and I need to intervene.

Action: This week I'll tell my son that he may no longer watch (or listen to)…

____ I'm concerned that my son may be depressed.

Action: During the next 24 hours, I will talk to my son about his feelings; if he seems truly depressed, I will make an appointment for the two of us to see…

3. Staying close

____ I need to be clearer about what the rules are in our home.

Action: This week I'll call a family meeting to discuss…

____ I do okay as a rule-giver, but I'm afraid the relationship isn't what it should be.

Action: This week I'll ask my spouse or a friend for an honest assessment of whether my behavior toward my son might be too…

___ I fear I'm losing track of my son and what he's doing.

Action: During the next 24 hours I'll sit down with my son and find out…

4. Gender identity

___ I have a hard time showing my son affection.

Action: During the next 24 hours I will give my son an around-the-shoulder hug whenever…

___ My son hears more criticism than approval from me.

Action: During the next 24 hours I will compliment him at least three times about…

___ I need to find a good male role model for my son.

Action: This week I will talk with a pastor or another man I trust to get suggestions on…

5. Spending time

____ I'm not spending enough time with my son.

Action: I will set aside the following block of time on the following day this week…

____ We spend time together, but I don't think he gets much out of it.

Action: This week I'll ask my son to make a list of the top ten things he'd like the two of us to do together, and then I'll…

____ I'm so busy that my life is out of control.

Action: This week I'll ask my spouse or a friend to help me slow down by cutting out…

6. Countering antimale bias

____ I need to talk with my son about antimale messages he sees on TV or in the movies.

Action: This week we'll watch and discuss…

____ My son's education is suffering because of antimale bias in the school system.

Action: This week I'll make an appointment to talk with the following teacher or administrator…

___ My son needs to learn more respect for himself and for the opposite sex.

Action: This week I'll model a respectful relationship with my spouse or, if I'm single, with an opposite-sex friend by…

7. Introducing your son to God

___ I need to take better advantage of "teachable moments" with my son.

Action: During the next 24 hours, I will look for at least two times when my son seems open to talking about…

___ I fear negative experiences at church or at home may be decreasing my son's interest in God.

Action: This week I'll ask my son to tell me honestly how he feels about…

___ I need to be more intentional about encouraging my son to accept Jesus as Savior.

Action: This week I'll call my son's Sunday school teacher, youth leader, or pastor, and ask how I could…

FOCUS ON THE FAMILY®

Welcome to the *Family!*

Whether you received this book as a gift, borrowed it from a friend, or purchased it yourself, we're glad you read it! It's just one of the many helpful, insightful, and encouraging resources produced by Focus on the Family.

In fact, that's what Focus on the Family is all about—providing inspiration, information, and biblically based advice to people in all stages of life.

It began in 1977 with the vision of one man, Dr. James Dobson, a licensed psychologist and author of 16 best-selling books on marriage, parenting, and family. Alarmed by the societal, political, and economic pressures that were threatening the existence of the American family, Dr. Dobson founded Focus on the Family with one employee—an assistant—and a once-a-week radio broadcast, aired on only 36 stations.

Now an international organization, Focus on the Family is dedicated to preserving Judeo-Christian values and strengthening the family through more than 70 different ministries, including eight separate daily radio broadcasts; television public service announcements; 13 publications; and a steady series of books and award-winning films and videos for people of all ages and interests.

Recognizing the needs of, as well as the sacrifices and important contribution made by, such diverse groups as educators, physicians, attorneys, crisis pregnancy center staff, and single parents, Focus on the Family offers specific outreaches to uphold and minister to these individuals, too. And it's all done for one purpose, and one purpose only: to encourage and strengthen individuals and families through the life-changing message of Jesus Christ.

• • •

For more information about the ministry, or if we can be of help to your family, simply write to Focus on the Family, Colorado Springs, CO 80995 or call 1-800-A-FAMILY (1-800-232-6459). Friends in Canada may write Focus on the Family, P.O. Box 9800, Stn. Terminal, Vancouver, B.C. V6B 4G3. or call 1-800-661-9800. Visit our Web site—www.family.org—to learn more about Focus on the Family or to find out if there is an associate office in your country.

We'd love to hear from you!

More Faith and Family Strengtheners
From Focus on the Family®

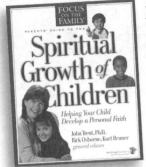

Parents' Guide to the Spiritual Growth of Children
Building a foundation of faith in your children can be easy and fun! Through simple and practical advice, *Parents' Guide to the Spiritual Growth of Children* will show you at what ages and stages you should be teaching your children different spiritual truths and principles. This guide will also help you customize a spiritual training plan for your family by providing ideas for entertaining family devotions, celebrations, and activities. Hardcover.

Parents' Guide to Teen Health
From raging hormones to unpredictable moods, teens face health challenges all their own. *Parents' Guide to Teen Health* helps parents support their teens as they navigate their way to adulthood. Encompassing physical, emotional, and spiritual issues, the guide gives wise counsel from more than 50 leading physicians, psychologists, and parenting experts. Paperback.

Creative Correction
If there's one thing that can wear parents out, it's that wonderful little word—*discipline*. Lisa Whelchel's (best known as "Blair" from the TV sitcom "The Facts of Life") *Creative Correction* is based on her own experiences with the never-ending challenge of correcting kids' behavior in a loving, yet effective, way. Covering the topics that concern parents most such as lying, sibling rivalry, and talking back, the book features a quick-reference index so you can get immediate help for your child's situation. If you're ready to get creative instead of frustrated, *Creative Correction* is the resource you've been waiting for. Hardcover.

●　●　●

Look for these special books in your Christian bookstore or request a copy by calling 1-800-A-FAMILY (1-800-232-6459). Friends in Canada may write Focus on the Family, P.O. Box 9800, Stn. Terminal, Vancouver, B.C. V6B 4G3 or call 1-800-661-9800.

Visit our Web site (www.family.org) to learn more about the ministry or find out if there is a Focus on the Family office in your country.